1607
A NEW LOOK AT
Jamestown

By Karen E. Lange
Photography by Ira Block
Foreword by Dr. William M. Kelso

NATIONAL GEOGRAPHIC

Washington, D.C.

To my children, Jeremy and Caroline,
and to their ancestors—German, Sicilian, French-Canadian, and Abenaki — KEL

In memory of my father, Norman Block — IB

Acknowledgments

Thanks to the Association for the Preservation of Virginia Antiquities (APVA) staff, especially Dr. William M. Kelso, director of archaeology, Beverly Straube, curator, Jamie May, archaeologist, and Catherine Correll-Walls, researcher; also to Dr. Martin Gallivan of the Werowocomoco Research Group, Dr. Edward Wright Haile, Dr. Carter Hudgins, Debby Padgett of Jamestown Settlement, Chief G. Anne Richardson of the Rappahannock tribe, and O.E. "Skip" Thomas of the Pepper Bird Foundation. Finally, I am grateful for the support of my husband, Stuart Gagnon, who took care of our children, ages one and six, while I was writing, and used his skills as a librarian to track down every book and article I asked for—and some I didn't even know existed.

Published by the National Geographic Society

John M. Fahey, Jr., *President and Chief Executive Officer*
Gilbert M. Grosvenor, *Chairman of the Board*
Nina D. Hoffman, *Executive Vice President, President of Books*

Staff for this Book

Nancy Laties Feresten, *Vice President, Editor-in-Chief, Children's Books*
Bea Jackson, *Director of Design and Illustrations, Children's Books*
Jennifer Emmett, Sue Macy, *Project Editors*
David M. Seager, *Art Director*
Lori Epstein, *Illustrations Editor*
Jean Cantu, *Illustrations Coordinator*
Priyanka Lamichhane, *Assistant Editor*
Carl Mehler, *Director of Maps*
Anne R. Gibbons, *Copy Editor*
Rebecca E. Hinds, *Managing Editor*
R. Gary Colbert, *Production Director*
Lewis R. Bassford, *Production Manager*
Vincent P. Ryan, Maryclare Tracy, *Manufacturing Managers*

The text of the book is set in Garamond.
The display text is Aquiline and Chanson d'Amour.

Trade ISBN: 978-1-4263-0012-7
Library ISBN: 978-1-4263-0013-4

Library of Congress Cataloging-in-Publication Data

Lange, Karen E.
  1607 : a new look at Jamestown / by Karen E. Lange ; photography by Ira Block.
    p. cm.
  Includes index.
  ISBN 1-4263-0012-3 (hardcover); ISBN 1-4263-0013-1 (library binding)
  1. Jamestown (Va.)—History—17th century. 2. Frontier and pioneer life—Virginia—Jamestown. 3. Powhatan Indians—Virginia—Jamestown—History—17th century. 4. Virginia—History—Colonial period, ca. 1600-1775. I. Title: New look at Jamestown. II. Title.
  F234.J3L37 2007
  973.2'1—dc22
                                                    2006005824

Illustrations Credits

All photos © Ira Block unless otherwise noted here.
Page 1: Virginia Historical Society. Page 3, 4-5, 6, 30, 44 (top): Richard T. Nowitz/Corbis. Page 8-9: Thomas L. Williams. Page 16-17, 20l (bottom), 29 (bottom), 37 (bottom), 40 (bottom): Association for the Preservation of Virginia Antiquities. Page 19: Joseph H. Baily. Page 27: Farrell Grehan. Page 32-33; George F. Mobley. Page 35: Bettmann/Corbis. Page 36: Nik Wheeler/Corbis. Page 42: David Muench/Corbis. Page 44 (bottom): Tim Wright.

Cover: An English settler holds his musket at the ready. The establishment of Jamestown began an on-again off-again war between the English and Virginia's Indians that lasted 60 years.

Title Page: Symbol of an uneasy friendship, a 17th-century silver medal issued by the English to a member of the Potomac tribe allowed the wearer to enter English settlements, but also identified him, in case he attacked the colonists.

Table of Contents: Navigational tools like those the English settlers used to cross the Atlantic and explore the Chesapeake Bay lie on top of an early map of the Americas.

Printed in the U.S.A.
  14/WOR/4

The costumed people shown in this book are actors interpreting the history of Jamestown.

Table of Contents

Foreword

Dr. William M. Kelso

Director of Archaeology for the Preservation of Virginia Antiquities (APVA)

Many people feel that to discover the past, all you have to do is find a book, open the pages, and read a single story. That couldn't be farther from the truth. History is not static: It is not a single story. Simple discovery may only yield you one layer. To really begin to understand the multi-faceted stories that make up our past, you must dig beyond what we think we know. You must discover and then re-discover.

That is what we are doing at Jamestown Rediscovery, one of the most important archaeological sites in the country. Jamestown is the birthplace of modern America. The settlers at Jamestown were the people who began to mold our sense of national identity. Understanding Jamestown is key to understanding how our nation came to be what it is today. Our language, our form of government, and our system of economics all have their roots at Jamestown.

Beginning in 1994, we were incredibly fortunate to uncover the 1607 James Fort, which most people thought had disappeared into the James River in the 18th century. Since then we've excavated more than one million artifacts to produce one of the largest collections of Early American Colonial artifacts in the world. Four hundred years after the founding of the colony, we now know more about Jamestown than we ever have, and we know that much of what we thought was so is not. It has been a tremendous rediscovery for me, this trip into the past.

In *1607: A New Look at Jamestown,* you have the opportunity for your own rediscovery as you take a new look at history, much as I do every day.

Only after many months did colonists construct houses within the 1607 fort. At first settlers slept in pits dug along the fort's walls and covered with canvas tarps.

Strangers in a Strange Land

*I*n the spring of 1607, after five months spent crossing the Atlantic Ocean, three small ships carrying 104 settlers from England reached North America. The voyagers landed on the coast of a land they called Virginia. Then they sailed up a river they named James, after their king. They searched for a good spot for a fort. The men and boys aboard the ships were risking their lives in a daring adventure: to found Jamestown, England's first permanent settlement in North America.

For decades, the English had tried but failed to establish colonies in North America. Settlers had died or given up or simply vanished: In 1590, a ship bringing supplies to an English colony on Roanoke Island, off the coast of present-day North Carolina, found the settlement mysteriously abandoned. The Roanoke colonists were never found.

Where the English had failed, the Spanish had succeeded. Spain had many colonies in the Americas and had grown rich and powerful from their gold. Spain had a settlement in Florida and claimed land up the east coast of the

---

The Susan Constant *and two smaller ships arrived in Jamestown after stopping in the Caribbean to take on fresh water and food. The colonists came ashore on a swampy peninsula, where the land juts into the James River (above).*

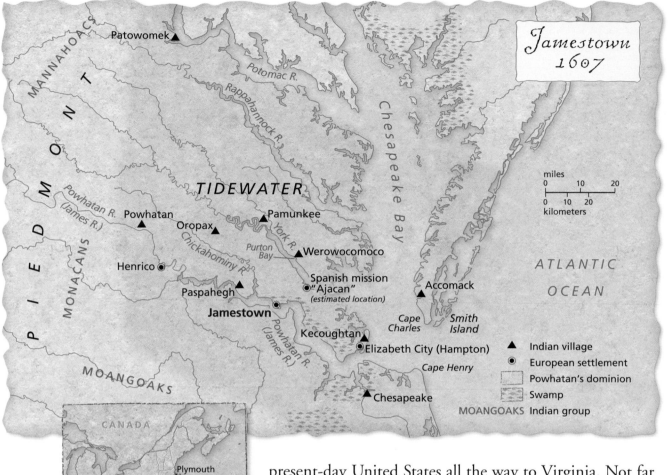

Jamestown lies in the Tidewater region of Virginia, which is bounded on the east by the Atlantic Ocean and on the west by an imaginary line that connects the first waterfalls along the rivers.

present-day United States all the way to Virginia. Not far from the James River, a small group of Spaniards had tried to start a town and Catholic mission in 1570. But they were killed by Indians.

The 104 colonists sailing up the James knew that if the king of Spain learned about their settlement, he might send his navy to destroy it and them. So they looked carefully for a place they could defend from Spanish ships. On May 15, the expedition's leaders found the spot they were looking for—a piece of land nearly surrounded by water 36 miles up the James River. They liked the site's position. It was connected to the mainland by only a narrow strip of ground. It lay next to a deep channel that allowed the English to tie their ships to trees on the shore. And it offered a nearby spot where lookouts could be posted to watch for the enemy.

But the site also had problems. It was low and marshy, with little dry land. And it was so close to the ocean that the water in the river tasted of salt. Worst of all, it had no freshwater springs or streams.

The settlers—well-dressed, high-ranking leaders called gentlemen, as well as soldiers, craftsmen, laborers, and four boys who came to learn trades—stepped ashore on a high stretch of ground along the island's northwest edge. They began lashing branches together to make a crude fort. As they worked in the mild air, perhaps swatting mosquitoes from the surrounding swamp, they did not know how much danger they faced. Under orders to be friendly to the Indians, they did not unpack their guns.

Within a year, two-thirds of the settlers would perish from hunger, disease, and Indian attacks. Within three years, as settlers continued to die in large numbers,

The English found plentiful timber around Jamestown to build their houses, which had walls made of sticks plastered with mud.

Jamestown was almost abandoned. The terrible death toll continued for almost 20 years, into the 1620s. By 1624, the business that had started the colony and tried to make a profit from it—the Virginia Company—had run out of money. The English king withdrew his permission for the company to operate the colony. Instead, Jamestown became a colony ruled directly by the king.

For generations, historians have blamed Jamestown's near failure on the foolishness and laziness of its planners, leaders, and ordinary settlers. "[They] appear to have been without a trace of foresight or enterprise," wrote W. E. Woodward in *A New American History,* published in 1937. "Though they were eating up their supply of food, they wandered about, looking over the country, and dreaming of gold mines. To dig a well for pure water would have been a labor of only a few hours, but they did not have the gumption to do that."

Now those views are changing. Archaeologists have located and begun excavating the site of Jamestown's earliest settlement—the 1607 fort. They have also discovered the capital of the ruler of the local Indian tribes, and have dug at smaller sites that reveal how Indians lived before and just after Europeans arrived. Scientists have figured out what Jamestown's climate was like around 1607. And researchers have found new records from the time that help explain events in the colony's early years.

It has taken four centuries, but we now have a better understanding of why so many died during Jamestown's early years. And from this we have a better understanding of the beginnings of the United States. Because, in many ways, the United States got its start at Jamestown.

Archaeologist Bill Kelso (standing) and a team of excavators found Jamestown's original, triangular fort in the 1990s. They first uncovered the eastern corner, where two walls held cannons.

A NATIVE AMERICAN EMPIRE

The land the English chose for Jamestown already belonged to someone else: It was used for hunting and fishing by an Indian tribe called the Paspaheghs. This tribe was one of around 30 in a powerful group of Indians. Historians call the group the Powhatan, after its ruler, a chief named Powhatan. The English at first believed they received permission from the Paspahegh chief to settle at Jamestown. Based on the hostilities that soon followed they were almost certainly wrong. More importantly, they did not have Powhatan's approval.

Most of Virginia between the ocean on the east and the first waterfalls along the rivers on the west looked like empty land to the English. But the region, called the Tidewater, was all claimed. The ancestors of the Powhatan had come to the region 1,400 years before—when Rome still ruled much of Europe. By 1600, perhaps as many as 25,000 Indians lived in the Tidewater region. Powhatan ruled about half of them. His empire covered 10,000 square miles of land and water, from where Interstate 95 now cuts through Virginia east to the ocean, south to North Carolina, and north to Maryland *(see map page 8)*.

English visitors praised the comfort of the houses of the Tidewater Indians (above), built of bent saplings covered with tightly woven mats that kept out the rain but did not lock in heat. Smoke from fires drove away insects (opposite).

The Indians' diet included a mix of foods, like this deer on a spit and the contents of this bowl: sunflower seeds, dried cherries, persimmons, dried fish called croaker, hominy corn, and dried pumpkin, squash, pinto beans, and mushrooms.

The Powhatan lived in villages and farmed. But their farming methods were different from English farming. The Indians planted a mix of crops—corn and beans and squash—all together in the same fields. They used digging sticks instead of plows. Their plots were small and often contained large trees left in place. The Indians had stone, not metal, axes, and so could not easily cut trees down.

The Powhatan also hunted and gathered to survive. During the spring and summer and fall, many would leave their villages in search of food. The small number of people in Indian villages during the warm months made Powhatan lands look uncrowded to the newly arrived English. But in reality the Indians were using every bit of space.

And other Indians were pressing in. To the north, tribes related to the Iroquois were coming down the Potomac River, raiding villages as they went. It was hard for the Powhatan to stop these invaders. The raiders had swift and silent birch bark canoes and metal hatchets they got by trading with the French. The Powhatan had only slow, heavy canoes dug out of logs and stone weapons. To the west, the Powhatan fought every year with two tribes called the Monacans and Mannahoacs. The Powhatan fortified towns against enemy arrows with screens of saplings and tree boughs.

The danger from the north and west helped Powhatan build his empire. Some tribes

In addition to copper, Indians around Jamestown traded with the English for blue glass beads. They resembled the beads the Indians made from clamshells, which were valuable and a sign of the wearer's wealth and prestige.

joined voluntarily, hoping Powhatan would protect them and fearing attacks by his warriors if they did not. Other tribes were forced into Powhatan's empire. His warriors killed their men and took their women and children prisoner.

Powhatan ruled from a capital called Werowocomoco, which lies on a bluff overlooking present-day Purton Bay along the York River north of Jamestown. There he and the chiefs over whom he ruled gathered.

When the English arrived, Powhatan and his chiefs did not necessarily see the "strangers" as enemies. Instead, they wondered whether they could use the English to help fight their enemies and to get objects they wanted: guns, axes, knives, and other metal weapons and tools.

The English had something else the Powhatan wanted even more than metal tools and weapons: copper. This metal was to the Indians what gold was to the English.

Powhatan controlled all the copper that came into his empire. He used it to pay the chiefs he ruled, who in turn used it to reward their best warriors. The copper was made into pendants and tubular beads and worn around Indians' necks and arms. When chiefs and warriors died, lavish amounts of copper were buried with them. Indians believed that its presence in the graves allowed their spirits to live on.

Around the time Jamestown's settlers arrived, Powhatan heard a frightening prediction. A priest told him that a nation from the Chesapeake Bay, which lies between the Virginia coast and the Atlantic, would destroy his empire. Powhatan thought this threat would come from other Indians, not Europeans. To the southeast of Powhatan's territory lived a tribe called the Chesapeake that had refused to join his empire. Powhatan sent his warriors to wipe out the Chesapeake. He ordered everyone slaughtered. Then he moved a tribe that was loyal to him onto the Chesapeake's land.

This was the world into which the English sailed.

All That Glitters

One of the most common items unearthed within Jamestown's 1607 fort during recent years is copper. Archaeologists led by William Kelso, of the Association for the Preservation of Virginia Antiquities (APVA), found more than 8,000 pieces there between 1994 and 2004. They ranged from tiny trimmings to larger sheets.

Artifacts from an Indian site six miles upriver show that the Jamestown copper was traded to the Powhatan. Graves in a 1607–09 Paspahegh village contained copper beads, pendants, and bracelets. Copper mined in different places and processed in different ways contains different chemicals. The chemicals in the Paspahegh copper match those of the Jamestown copper. All of the copper came from England.

Archaeologists can tell how much trade was going on between the English and Indians by counting artifacts. Excavators dug up a lot of copper artifacts in deposits that date from 1607 through 1609. Scholar Seth Mallios thinks the large number of copper artifacts dating back to Jamestown's founding show that a lot of trade was going on then. But the amount of copper drops off at sites from 1610 on. Mallios thinks this is because the English traded so much copper to the Indians that the metal lost its value.

Copper may also have been shipped to Jamestown as a raw material for brass. Copper and zinc combined make brass, used to manufacture cannons. England had the right kind of copper for brass, but not the right kind of zinc. Scholar Carter Hudgins thinks settlers who worked with melted copper in thick-walled clay beakers called crucibles were trying to produce the right kind of zinc for brass.

Archaeologists at Jamestown dug up round copper jettons that were used in mathematical calculations and copper rolled into tubular beads or cut into pendants.

NOTHING TO LOSE

England in the early 1600s was a good place to leave. People were being forced off land they farmed and into poverty. Once, most families had tilled small plots that belonged to wealthy property owners called lords. In return for the right to farm the land, families gave part of their harvests to these lords. But in the early 1600s this way of life, called *feudalism*, was breaking down. Property owners were selling and renting their land. Landlords were driving away families who could not afford to lease or buy fields. Often property owners fenced off large areas, including land that had been shared by all, to make money from businesses like sheep farming.

Just as families were being thrown off farms, the number of people living in England was increasing. So in the countryside, there was not enough land. In the cities, there were not enough jobs. The landless, jobless, and hungry wandered from place to place looking for a way to survive. England's rich feared these "vagrants." In order to stop them from wandering about, the country's rulers

---

Many early Jamestown settlers came from London and from communities along England's south and east coasts long linked to shipbuilding and the sea (opposite). They were drawn by the promise of land and homes to call their own (above).

Jamestown's many high-ranking gentlemen displayed their status through the way they dressed, in touches as small as silver buttons (right) or an ornate combination tooth and ear pick that could be worn on a chain (below).

locked up the poor and homeless. They sent them to orphanages, prisons, and workhouses, where they labored long days for a little food.

Many of the people who settled Jamestown were poor, with few opportunities in England. About half of the earliest settlers were indentured servants— craftsmen and laborers who paid for their ship passage by promising to work for five to seven years without pay.

Most of the rest of the settlers during Jamestown's early years came from wealthy, high-ranking families that owned land—the gentlemen. In England they had a special status that allowed them to help the king to govern and required lower-ranking people to obey them. To let everyone know how important they were, gentlemen wore fancy clothes. They wore coats with silver-braided threads, collars pressed with scores of ruffles, and gold-plated spurs—even when they weren't riding horses.

They paid their own way across the Atlantic and received food and clothing from their families on later supply ships.

Jamestown's gentlemen went to Virginia to serve God and their country and to get rich. They hoped to convert the Indians to Christianity and to win a part of the New World for England. They also hoped to find new sources of raw materials and an easy way to reach Asia by ship.

Most of the Jamestown gentlemen had two, three, or more older brothers. Because they were not born first or second, they would not inherit their families' money or businesses. In England such young men often agreed to apprentice to artisans, merchants, ship captains, or military officers. But these younger sons had chosen adventure instead.

Gentlemen were among the few settlers who knew how to shoot a musket. In England only people who belonged to the highest-ranking classes could afford firearms. Most hunted regularly with guns. Many of Jamestown's gentlemen were also soldiers with military experience. As the settlement's military force, they built and guarded the fort and protected groups that went exploring.

Though criticized as lazy, gentlemen were among the only colonists who knew how to use guns (top), since low-ranking people rarely owned firearms in England. Gentlemen defended the colony and hunted for food with round bullets called musket balls (above).

Captain John Smith, one of the few leaders of Jamestown who was not a gentleman, did not think much of these high-ranking settlers. He accused them of refusing to work with the rest of the colonists. He complained that there were too many gentlemen at Jamestown. He wrote to the Virginia Company, pleading, "I [beg] you rather send but 30 carpenters, husbandmen, gardeners, fishermen, blacksmiths, masons, and diggers-up of trees' roots … than a thousand of such as we have."

Instead the company sent foreign experts—Poles, Dutch, Germans, French, Italians, Welsh, and Irish—to make glass, wine, and silk, and to look for gold and other precious metals. The Virginia Company needed colonists to ship back valuable commodities to England. It also wanted the colonists to trade with the Indians for food. Reports from the failed colony at Roanoke had described how much the Indians valued copper, so the company sent settlers with a lot of it to trade.

The company planned for the Indians to provide not only the food for Jamestown but also much of the labor. In return the Indians would receive Christianity, civilization, and good government. The English thought this would be a fair exchange.

A few of the settlers arriving in every supply ship during Jamestown's early years were boys. In England at that time, children often were sent to live as apprentices or servants and to get an education. In the same way, families sent boys to Jamestown as servants and apprentices so they could learn a trade or find their fortunes.

Because of their ages, these boys were better at learning languages than adult settlers. The colony's leaders used

English armor could stop stone-tipped Indian arrows but it was hot and heavy to wear. The settlers adapted by cutting armor into small pieces and quilting the metal into arrow-proof vests. They carried gunpowder in cylinders called bandoliers.

them to build friendships with the Indians. They gave English boys to chiefs as pledges of good faith. Living among the Indians, the boys became fluent speakers of the Powhatan tongue. They translated for both sides.

One such interpreter was 13-year-old Henry Spelman. Spelman wrote that he left England, "being in displeasure of my friends, and desirous to see other countries." He went to Jamestown as a laborer but was traded to one of chief Powhatan's sons for a piece of land. He arrived among the Indians when the friendship between the English and Powhatan was breaking down. After he watched the Indians skin a captured English officer alive with a razor-sharp clam shell, Spelman ran away. As he fled, he almost had his head bashed in with a stone axe. Shipping off to Virginia was a risky business.

Shipped to Jamestown to learn trades and serve as pages to gentlemen, boys were often swept into the battles between the English and the Indians. Some, sent to live with the Indians, in time learned the Indian language and helped the two sides understand each other.

Indians at the Fort

When archaeologists found a lot of "arrowheads," or projectile points, inside Jamestown's 1607 fort, they weren't surprised. The broken points were from arrows shot into the fort during Indian attacks. The unbroken ones were gifts from the Indians to the English. But archaeologists were surprised by other finds: half-made projectile points, tools for working stone, and flakes left over from chipping stone into points. All are clues that Indians may have lived at the fort.

Excavators also found Indian pottery—thin-walled vessels made of clay mixed with bits of shells. Most of the pots were round-bottomed, designed to be set in a hearth for cooking. Some of them contained bits of food—corn and deer. In one such pot archaeologists discovered the remains of a turtle. Nearby, they found a type of blue glass bead the English traded to the Powhatan, along with a stone hammer and a dagger in a sheath. Curator Beverly Straube, who studies artifacts dug up at the fort, believes these objects might have been left behind by an Indian woman cooking for one of the English men.

In 1612, the Spanish ambassador to England reported to his king that 40 to 50 English men at Jamestown had married Indian women. These relationships helped foster peace and understanding. From 1609 to 1610, 100 English women arrived in Jamestown. During that time fighting between the English and Indians increased. Straube says it's no coincidence: The arrival of English women may have upset relationships between English men and Powhatan women and led Powhatan to understand the English were there to stay.

Meals cooked in Indian pots found in colonists' houses show that Indian women may have lived at the fort with English men during the early years at Jamestown.

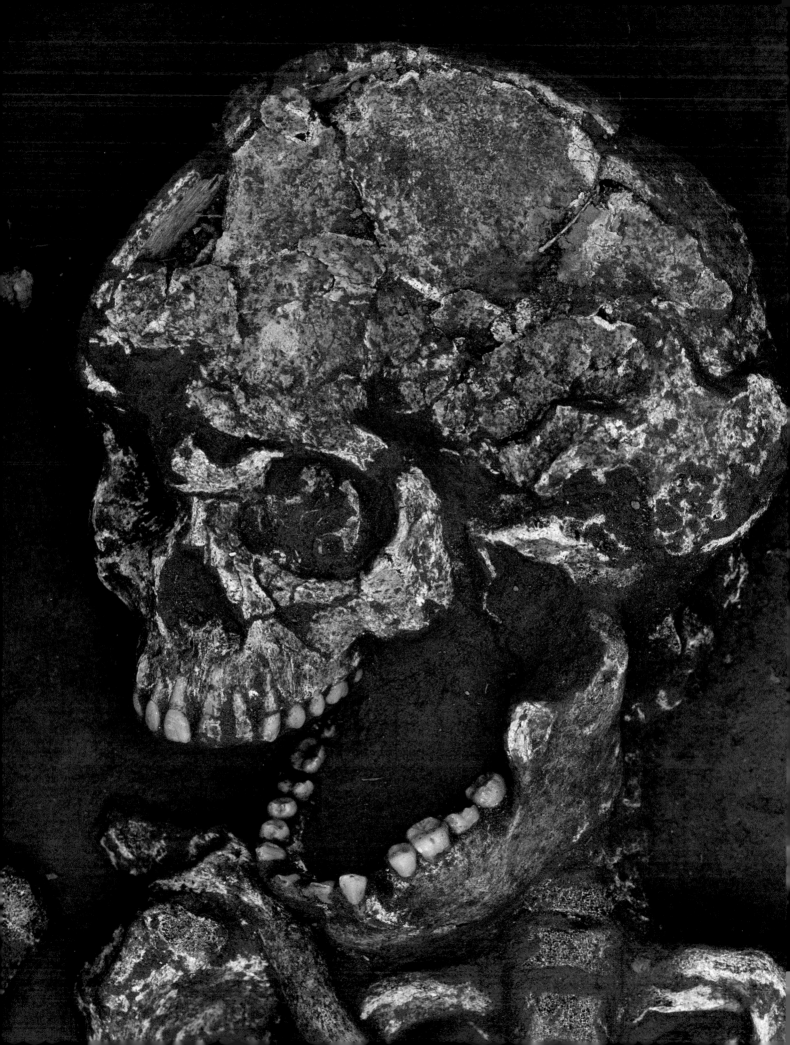

THE DYING TIMES

Within days of the settlers' landing in 1607, hundreds of Powhatan warriors attacked. We do not know exactly why, but we can guess. Chief Powhatan did not have absolute control over the tribes within his empire. One or more of the chiefs under Powhatan may have been offended by the English. The strangers had taken Paspahegh land. They had threatened Powhatan visitors with weapons.

While a party of settlers was away exploring up the river, the Indians surprised the remaining colonists. The English had been planting corn. Retreating from a rain of arrows, the settlers fell back in confusion. As the Indians chased the English to the entrance of the fort, sailors aboard the ships fired cannons at the attackers. Had it not been for the cannon fire, wrote Captain John Smith, "our men [would have] all been slain." As it was, one of the English boys was killed and at least eleven English men were wounded.

Immediately, Jamestown's first president, Edward Maria Wingfield, ordered the settlers to surround the fort with 12-foot-high walls made of split or unhewn timber

---

An early gentlemen settler whose skeleton (opposite) was found in the 1607 fort probably died of a gunshot wound to the leg. Many more colonists, who crowded into the fort (above) to escape Indian attacks, died of hunger and disease.

Settlers at Jamestown caught fatal diseases when they drank from the salty, polluted river. Strict rules forbade colonists from fouling wells like this one.

planted in the ground. The men completed these palisades in a month of furious work. They put cannons in the triangular fort's three corners. Warned by friendly Indians, the English cut the grass around the walls. The grass had allowed warriors to creep close to the settlement unseen and shoot arrows at colonists who ventured outside.

On June 15, after a month of raids, Powhatan ordered his warriors to stop. Then the great chief started sending Jamestown gifts of deer meat.

When Captain Christopher Newport left Jamestown on June 22 to sail back to England for more supplies, the colony's future seemed good. His ship held a cargo of timber that the settlers had cut in the woods around the fort. The Indians were suddenly friendly. Settlers sent back glowing reports. "Now is the King's Majesty offered the most stately, rich kingdom in the world, never possessed by any Christian prince," wrote a gentlemen named William Brewster.

But a few weeks later, Brewster and many others died. Colonist George Percy recorded the first of the deaths: "Our men were destroyed with cruel diseases— as swellings [bloody diarrhea], burning fevers—and by wars. Some departed suddenly, but for the most part they died of mere famine." There were 104 colonists in May 1607. By January 1608 only 38 remained alive.

John Smith and other eyewitnesses blamed the deaths on foolish, quarrelsome leaders and settlers who didn't know how to farm or fish and didn't want to try. Jamestown's leaders frequently argued and plotted against each other. Even before

By studying the remains of early settlers (above) archaeologists hope to figure out why so many died. Below: A U-shaped musket rest that fit on a pole to help a hunter aim his gun; a bandolier cylinder, or container for gunpowder; and a hook and lead weights for fishing testify to the colonists' struggle to feed themselves.

they got off their ships, Smith was placed under arrest for insulting President Wingfield. Once ashore, Jamestown's leaders mistrusted each other. They shot Captain George Kendall as a Spanish spy. For their part, Jamestown's ordinary colonists appeared to slack off after the first months of hard work building a fort.

But even if Jamestown had had the best leaders and settlers, it would have been difficult for them to survive. Percy identified the problem early on: The colonists were drinking from a salty, polluted river. "Our drink [was] cold water taken out of the river, which was at a flood very salt, at a low tide full of slime and filth," he wrote.

The settlers arrived at Jamestown just before summer, the season when the river is the saltiest and most polluted. Some settlers who drank the river water suffered from salt poisoning. They became tired and irritable and their bodies swelled up. Others fell sick because of bacteria in the water. They came down with dysentery—a severe and often bloody diarrhea—and typhoid fever.

The first of several wells was dug in 1608, under Smith's order. Later, to protect these wells and people's general health, Jamestown's leaders forbade settlers from going to the bathroom or dumping the waste they collected in chamber pots

Sailors stored fish on board ship by salting it. Colonists were more successful at fishing and collecting shellfish such as oysters than at hunting deer, for which they relied on Indian expertise.

within the fort. Colonists had to walk at least a quarter mile away (sometimes dodging arrows). But either the wells were too shallow to reach good water or the river seeped in. Perhaps the settlers ignored the rules. Colonists continued to get sick and die as long as they remained at Jamestown.

If the colonists had picked the wrong place to settle, they had also picked the wrong time. Drought struck from 1607 through 1612, withering crops like corn.

Irregular supply ships brought rations of barley, barreled meat, butter, peas, and other food for the colonists. The settlers also caught fish such as sturgeon, shot ducks and other fowl, and gathered oysters. But much of their food came through trade with the Indians. John Smith wrote that he once traded 25 pounds of copper, 50 pounds of iron, and blue glass beads for enough bread, corn, meat, fowl, and fish to feed 40 men for six months. The drought upset this trade.

Even during times of normal rainfall, the Powhatan did not have much extra corn to trade to the English. They raised only enough to feed themselves and pay tribute to chief Powhatan. When rains failed, the Indians themselves went hungry. The Powhatan could not keep providing food to the English. Desperate, the English threatened to seize food if the Indians would not give it to them.

To make matters worse, the Indians no longer wanted the copper the settlers were offering. That's probably because the English, especially sailors docked at Jamestown, had flooded the market with copper. They gave the Indians so much that the metal became common and lost its value.

Beset by English demands for their food and no longer wishing to trade with the settlers, the Powhatan tried to drive their new neighbors away. They sent English men living with them back to Jamestown and surrounded the fort with warriors. Inside, the settlers drank bad water, fell sick, and went hungry. With no other food, they ate dogs, cats, horses, rats, and even poisonous snakes.

"Many through extreme hunger [ran] out of their naked beds, being so lean they looked like [skeletons], crying out 'We are starved! We are starved!'" wrote George Percy. "Others going to bed, as we imagined, in health, were found dead the next morning."

Malnourished, weak from disease, isolated, and hopeless, some of the settlers gave up on life. Though they were not starving or seriously ill, they lay down and died.

Altogether during the "starving time" winter and spring of 1609 to 1610, about 100 of an estimated 200 colonists perished. Jamestown's settlers had remained through three years of disease, hunger, and death. But the intense suffering of the "starving time" left the survivors ready to quit and go home. They boarded the first ship to reach Jamestown and were sailing away when they met another ship. It was carrying the colony's new governor and supplies. The settlers turned back to try again.

Archaeologists uncovered an early cemetery that provides evidence of Jamestown's high death rate. During the worst times, when scores perished quickly, settlers buried them in haphazardly dug holes, sometimes dropping more than one body in a grave.

Discovering the Drought

If archaeologists want to know how much it rained hundreds of years ago, they often turn to trees. Each of the rings visible on a tree stump marks a year's worth of growth. Rings at the center show growth during the earliest years of a tree's life. Those at the outer edge show more recent growth.

When trees get enough rain, they grow a lot. Growth layers are thick and rings are spaced wide apart. When trees do not get enough rain, they grow very little. Growth layers are thin and rings appear close together.

To figure out how much rain fell during the early years at Jamestown, scientists had to find trees that were alive there in 1607. Fortunately those trees exist. Bald cypress trees growing around Jamestown are centuries old. The scientists bored narrow holes into these trees to extract cores that showed all the growth layers from the cypress's bark to their centers. Then, starting from the trees' outermost rings, the scientists counted back in time. When they reached the period during which Jamestown was first settled, they were astounded: The rings laid down from 1606 to 1612 were among the narrowest of all.

It must have rained very little during those years for the trees to grow so little, archaeologist Dennis B. Blanton and scientist David W. Stahle reported in 1998. The scientists decided that the seven-year period from 1606 to 1612 was the driest in almost eight centuries.

A cross section of a tree reveals the past. Years of little rain led to narrow growth layers in this drought-stressed tree, while wet periods made a series of wide rings.

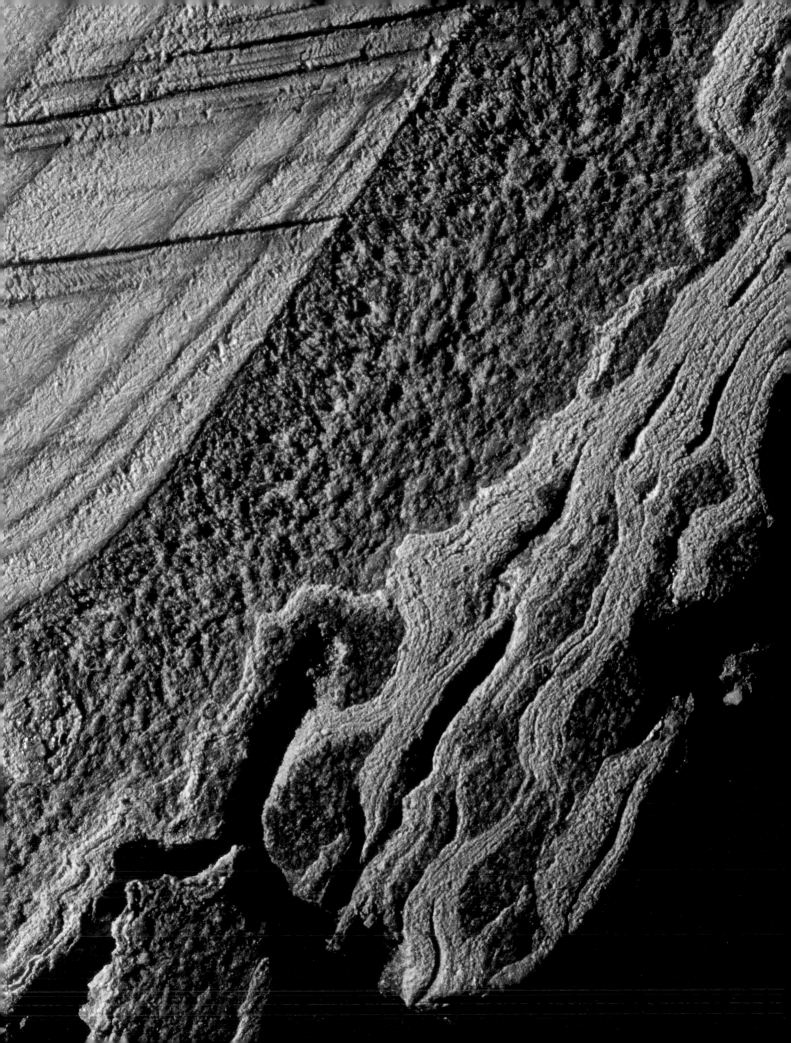

GREEN GOLD

By 1610, Jamestown seemed a total failure. Hundreds of its settlers were dead and all its money-making schemes in ruins. Then a man arrived who would change everything: John Rolfe.

The tobacco grown by the Indians in Virginia burned the throats of those who smoked it. Rolfe found a milder strain of tobacco on Trinidad, a Caribbean island far to the south of Virginia. In 1611, he brought this sweeter-tasting tobacco to Virginia. Soon Rolfe figured out the best way to grow it, and started selling tobacco to pipe smokers in England.

Tobacco took off. So many people wanted to grow it that colonists stopped planting crops to eat. By 1618, colonists were shipping more than 50,000 pounds of tobacco to England. The colony was finally turning a profit.

Originally, all the colony's land had belonged to the Virginia Company. But little by little, to encourage people to come to Virginia and to reward hard work, the company gave settlers their own pieces of property to farm. When the tobacco boom

Tobacco was the get-rich-quick crop that saved Jamestown. Settlers could plant in peace because of the marriage of John Rolfe to Pocahontas (above) daughter of a powerful Indian chief. This 1616 portrait shows her on a visit to England.

If the indentured servants who did most of Jamestown's labor lived long enough, they received freedom and often money and land. But their service was hard. Their masters could beat them and work them to exhaustion. A ship captain wrote that servants were bought and sold "like horses."

hit, the company gave free settlers—those who were not indentured servants—who were already in Virginia 100 acres of land. In addition, anyone who paid his or another's way to Virginia got 50 acres of land. And anyone who bought a share in the company got 100 acres of land.

These changes allowed rich people to start huge tobacco plantations. Soon colonists had established about 40 of these plantations up and down the James River. They turned more and more Powhatan land into tobacco farms.

The settlers were able to do this because a colonist and an Indian had fallen in love. In 1613, the colonists took Pocahontas, one of chief Powhatan's daughters, hostage, hoping to trade her for English prisoners held by the Indians. Her father refused. So Pocahontas, then about 18, remained with the English. John Rolfe began to spend a lot of time with her. In a letter he wrote that she had captured his heart and he could think of no one else. The two married in 1614, and from that time until Pochahontas's death in 1617, the English and Indians were at peace.

To work the plantations established during the "Peace of Pocahontas," landowners needed many, many people. They paid for lots of men and women to come to Virginia from England. In return, these new arrivals had to work for the landowners for seven years as indentured servants. The type of slavery that would later take root in Virginia did not yet exist. In 1619, only about 50 of 1,000 settlers were Africans. Thirty-two African "servants" lived in the colony at the start of the year. Around 20 slaves from southwestern Africa (now Angola) arrived later, by accident. They had been captured from a Portuguese slave ship by Dutch pirates. The pirates stopped at Jamestown and traded the Africans for supplies.

To convince more English to come and stay in the colony, the Virginia Company gave colonists a voice in their government. For many years settlers had lived under strict, military-style rules called martial law. Now the company

Women were sent to Jamestown as wives, to cook and clean and wash clothes for settler men. They also planted gardens, reducing the colony's dependence on Indian-grown corn. (Shown below is a 400-year-old bit of cob excavated by archaeologists.)

relaxed those rules. It allowed colonists who owned land to elect representatives. Each part of the colony sent two representatives to an assembly called the House of Burgesses, which met for the first time in 1619. These representatives passed laws and helped govern Virginia. This was the start of democracy in America.

To keep men in the colony the Virginia Company also tried increasing the number of women. The company thought that married men would be happier—less likely to run off to live with the Indians or go home to England. So in 1619 it launched the "Maids for Virginia" program, which sent 147 women to marry the colony's gentlemen.

The maids were women of high social rank in their teens and 20s. Investors paid for the maids' passages, clothing, and supplies. The investors hoped to get back their money and more: Each man wishing to marry a "young, handsome, and honestly educated maid" had to give the company 150 pounds of the best tobacco.

As wives, these women prepared meals, cleaned, sewed, and laundered. For many years the settlement had been run like an army outpost, with filthy housing and bad food. Now it became a colony of families, with children.

By the 1620s, it was clear to the Virginia Indians that Jamestown was no small trading post. Pocahontas's marriage to John Rolfe had kept the peace, but now she was dead. At the end of a visit to England, just after she boarded a ship to return to Virginia, she became ill from what may have been consumption, or tuberculosis. She died within days. Chief Powhatan himself died a year after his daughter. A new chief named Opechancanough became leader of the Powhatan. He was determined to drive the English out of Virginia.

WINNERS TAKE ALL

By 1622, after eight years of peace, English and Indians were living side by side in much of the Tidewater. Indians traded at Jamestown and English plantations. Settlers hunted with Powhatan guides. Some English lived in Powhatan villages, and some Powhatan lived with the English.

So on the morning of March 22, 1622, settlers did not take much notice of the many Indians who drifted into the colony's plantations. The warriors were there on the orders of Opechancanough, ruler of the Powhatan. They struck suddenly, killing 347 settlers. The colony lost a quarter of its population. Jamestown was spared only because an Indian friendly to the English warned colonists there.

Hunger and disease were still taking many English lives in the 1620s, and conditions got worse after the massacre. Reeling from the attack, many of the surviving settlers on plantations retreated to Jamestown. There they lived in the same unhealthy conditions that had sickened and killed the first colonists. Ships arriving from England also brought disease—like the plague and dysentery, or

---

When colonists let down their guard, they were massacred by Indians fighting to reclaim the land. Indian arrows could go clean through a shield like this one (above).

Muskets gave the settlers an edge over the Indians because lead shot (right, shown cast in a mold) could fire 70 to 100 yards, while arrows could travel only 40. But a warrior might shoot five arrows while a colonist paused to reload.

40

"the bloody flux." And food was in short supply. Farmers faced attack, and settlers could no longer trade for corn with the Powhatan.

"[We] must work hard both early and late for a mess of water gruel and a mouthful of bread and beef," wrote Richard Frethorne, an indentured servant in 1623 on a plantation called Martin's Hundred. "We live in fear of the enemy every hour." Within a year Frethorne himself died.

The Virginia Company sent reinforcements and declared all-out war on the Powhatan. The English saw the Indians as enemies to be driven out of the Tidewater and captured as slaves. "[We] may now by right of war, and law of nations, invade the country, and destroy who sought to destroy us," declared Edward Waterhouse, an English writer.

The colonists showed no mercy. When an English captain was invited to peace talks at a Powhatan village in 1623, he and his men went plotting murder. He put poison in the drink used to toast the treaty, killing 200 Indians. Then the English slew 50 of the survivors.

The Powhatan steadily lost ground to the English. In 1644, there was another big Powhatan attack against English settlements, with 400 to 500 men, women, and children killed. But it was the last. English people continued to take Powhatan land. In 1677, the Powhatan signed a peace treaty that gave them reservation lands in return for annual payments to Virginia's governor. The tribute payments take place to this day.

It is not that the governor wants or needs the deer meat the Indians bring him. It is that both sides want to remember and honor the past. For Virginia's Indians, the ceremony is especially important. They have had to struggle to maintain their culture and identity, and their claims to reservation land. In the 1970s and 1980s they had to fight for official state recognition as tribes. Each November they remind the governor and the rest of Virginia that they are still here.

A New Look at Jamestown

At first there were plans to mark Jamestown's 400th anniversary in 2007 with a celebration. Then Virginia Indians spoke up. For the Indians, Jamestown is nothing to celebrate. To them, it meant the end of their ancestors' way of life. So instead, the anniversary organizers planned for a time of remembering—a commemoration. But how should we remember Jamestown?

Plymouth, Massachusetts, has long been honored as the beginning of our country, even though that settlement was founded 13 years after Jamestown. On Thanksgiving, Americans remember the mythical legacy of Plymouth's God-fearing, hard-working Pilgrims. By comparison, Jamestown is overlooked.

Now the 2007 anniversary and recent discoveries have focused new attention on Jamestown. It is finally being honored as the foundation of our nation. Virginians are even saying that the real first thanksgiving took place in their state: In 1619, two years before the famous 1621 meal at Plymouth, settlers at Berkeley plantation on the James River held a feast to thank God for their safe arrival.

Yet the story of Jamestown is not a comforting one. It is not the happy myth

---

A statue of John Smith, the most famous of the settlers, stands at the site of the 1607 fort he helped build and defend. A short distance up the river, at a state park, reenactors like this blacksmith (above) teach visitors about Jamestown.

of Pilgrims planting the seeds of liberty, all the while helped by friendly Indians. Rather, it is a true story of suffering, of cruelty between English and Indians, and of thousands of unnecessary deaths. About three-quarters of those who went to Jamestown between 1607 and 1625—most of them young people—were dead by the end of the period. Jamestown colonists fought the first of many wars that forced native peoples off their land. They started the first of many plantations that would eventually bring slavery to the South.

But if the worst of America came from Jamestown, the best was also born there. In the colony's grim early years, even the gentlemen John Smith complained about were forced to labor with servants as equals—it was a matter of survival. Jamestown was a place where the poor might become rich through hard work, where people could govern themselves, and where cultures mixed to create a new, American way of life. When the Powhatan and English weren't killing each other, they shared ideas. This exchange was recorded in the language they spoke. Here are some of the words the English borrowed from the Powhatan, along with their Indian (Algonquin) origins: moccasin (*makasin*), tomahawk (*tamehakan*), raccoon (*araughcoon*), opossum (*aposum*), and pecan (*pakawn*).

Most of all, Jamestown is a story about not giving up—about persevering. The settlers could have quit. But instead they stayed on through sickness, hunger, war, and death. Four centuries after the first English stepped ashore, Americans still struggle with difficult problems. Sometimes they seem impossible to solve. Jamestown is a story of what can happen if people keep trying. From Jamestown, a colony that nearly failed, grew a great nation.

An interpreter dressed like a 17th-century gentleman tells 21st-century Americans about their forebears at Jamestown, while children try their hand at quoit, a colonial-era game of horseshoes.

Chronology

1550s–1607/08: Powhatan inherits the leadership of a small group of Indian tribes and builds it into an empire of some 30 tribes that covers most of what is now eastern Virginia.

1588–1604: Protestant England and Catholic Spain battle each other during 16 years of war on both sides of the Atlantic.

1590: An English colony established on Roanoke Island (present-day North Carolina) five years earlier is found abandoned, its settlers missing.

1607: Three ships sent by the Virginia Company of London bring the first settlers from England to Jamestown. To the north, settlers trying to establish an English colony at Popham, Maine, quit and go home.

1609–1610: So many Jamestown settlers die during the "starving time" winter that the colony is almost abandoned. Only the arrival of a new leader—Lord de la Warr—with supplies and new settlers convinces the survivors to remain

1611: Newly arrived settler John Rolfe introduces a milder and soon to be immensely popular type of tobacco to Virginia. Henrico and Elizabeth City—the first settlements beyond Jamestown—are established.

1613: Colonists kidnap Pocahontas, one of Powhatan's daughters, in an unsuccessful attempt to trade her for English men held prisoner by the Indians.

1614: Rolfe marries Pocahontas, beginning a peace between Indians and English. The truce will last through Pocahontas's sudden death in 1617 from an unidentified sickness.

1616: The Virginia Company states that it will grant 50 acres of land to anyone who pays for his own or another's passage.

1618: More than 50,000 pounds of tobacco are shipped back to England. Plantations are being founded up and down the James River. Powhatan dies.

1619: The House of Burgesses, or General Assembly, begins meeting, marking the start of representative government in the Western Hemisphere. The Virginia Company launches a program that will send 147 high-ranking women to Virginia to become the wives of gentlemen.

1622: A surprise attack by Powhatan Indians under the command of Opechancanough kills 347 Europeans in outlying settlements—at least a quarter of the colony's population.

1624: King James I revokes the bankrupt Virginia Company's charter and takes direct control of Jamestown and other Virginia settlements.

1644: The last big Powhatan attack kills 400 to 500 Europeans living on plantations outside Jamestown. Opechancanough is captured, then shot by the soldier guarding him.

1661: Slavery is recognized by law.

1676: Angered by Indian attacks and the colonial government's restrictions on westward expansion, settlers in Virginia's backcountry take up arms against the Powhatan and their own leaders. The Indians suffer huge losses and sign a treaty the next year, promising peace in return for reservations. The rebellion is eventually put down, but not before Jamestown is partially burned.

Stone projectile points or arrowheads, like the kind made by Virginia Indians are still plowed up in the state's farm fields and found scattered in the woods.

Bibliography

PRIMARY SOURCE MATERIAL

In order to help readers understand quotes from the early 1600s, I have corrected non-standard spellings and punctuation and given modern definitions [in brackets] for archaic words.

Jamestown Narratives: Eyewitness Accounts of the Virginia Colony; The First Decade: 1607-1617, edited with commentary by Edward Wright Haile, Roundhouse, 1998.

Everything written by those who experienced the settlement's early years, with introductions that explain the background and biases of each writer.

The Complete Works of Captain John Smith (1580-1631) in Three Volumes, edited by Philip L. Barbour, Volume 1, for Institute of Early American History and Culture, Williamsburg, Va., by University of North Carolina Press, 1986.

All the reports produced by Jamestown's best known, least modest, and most controversial figure. For generations, scholars doubted the accuracy of Smith's dramatic and sometimes contradictory accounts. Starting in the 1950s, Philip Barbour and later others argued that Smith was reliable more often than not.

www.virtualJamestown.org
(Click on "First Hand Accounts and Letters")

BOOKS

Jamestown Rediscovery: 1994-2004, by William M. Kelso and Beverly Straube, Association for the Preservation of Virginia Antiquities, 2004.

A summary of what was unearthed during the first decade of excavations at the site of the earliest Jamestown settlement.

The Virginia Adventure, Roanoke to Jamestown: An Archaeological and Historical Odyssey, by Ivor Noel Hume, Alfred A. Knopf, 1994.

An account of what was known about Jamestown before 1994 by the father of historical archaeology in the United States.

A Land as God Made It: Jamestown and the Birth of America, by James Horn, Basic Books, 2005.

An up-to-date history.

Jamestown and the Founding of the Nation, by Warren M. Billings, Thomas Publications, Gettysburg, 1995.

A short overview.

Pocahontas's People: The Powhatan Indians of Virginia Through Four Centuries, by Helen C. Rountree, University of Oklahoma Press, 1990.

Before and After Jamestown: Virginia's Powhatans and Their Predecessors, by Helen C. Rountree and E. Randolph Turner III, University Press of Florida, 2002.

Pocahontas, Powhatan, Opechancanough: Three Indian Lives Changed by Jamestown, by Helen C. Rountree, University of Virginia Press, 2005.

Three books that give the Indian perspective on Jamestown. The first is a history; the second puts more emphasis on prehistory and archaeology; the third tells the story through the eyes of three famous Powhatan figures.

American Slavery, American Freedom: The Ordeal of Colonial Virginia, by Edmund S. Morgan, W. W. Norton & Company, 1975.

A classic work on the development of slavery in Virginia.

Envisioning an English Empire: Jamestown and the Making of the North Atlantic World, edited by Robert Appelbaum and John Wood Sweet, University of Pennsylvania Press, 2005.

The perspectives of a variety of scholars.

Web Sites / Places to Visit

www.apva.org
Jamestown Rediscovery
Association for the Preservation of Virginia Antiquities (APVA)
1367 Colonial Parkway
Jamestown, Va.   23081

The actual site of the 1607 fort—22 ½ acres where archaeologists have been excavating since 1994. Artifacts are on display.

www.nps.gov/colo/
Colonial National Historical Park
(National Park Service)

The 1,500-acre island surrounding the fort site, including Jamestown's later "New Towne."

www.historicjamestowne.org
Historic Jamestowne
(757) 229-0412 (APVA) or (757) 229-1733 (National Park Service)
The jointly administered APVA and National Park Service property.

www.historyisfun.org
Jamestown Settlement
(Commonwealth of Virginia)
Route 31 and Colonial Parkway
Jamestown-Yorktown Foundation
P.O. Box 1607
Williamsburg, Va.   23187
(757) 253-4838 or (888) 593-4682

Reconstructions of a Powhatan Indian village, the ships that brought the 1607 settlers, and James Fort, located just upriver from the actual site of Jamestown. Costumed interpreters reenact daily life. A museum displays period artifacts. The reenactment pictures for this book were taken there.

www.virtualJamestown.org

A growing collection of primary sources, essays, maps, watercolors and engravings, and other information related to Jamestown.

http://powhatan.wm.edu/
Werowocomoco Research Project

News of the excavation of the Powhatan capital, recently discovered on a private farm.

www.Indians.vipnet.org
Virginia Council on Indians

Eight of the tribes the English settlers met in the early 1600s continue to exist and are recognized by the Commonwealth of Virginia.

www.pepperbird.com/va/indian/
Pepper Bird Foundation
P.O. Box 1071
Williamsburg, Va.   23187-1071
(800) 496-1973

Offers listings of powwows and other events, museums, and sites related to Virginia Indians, past and present.

Sources for Quotes & Information

Full citations are given the first time a source is mentioned, and abbreviated ones after that. Books listed as primary sources in the bibliography are referred to in abbreviated form.

Strangers in a Strange Land
page 11: Woodward (*A New American History,* by W.E. Woodward, Literary Guild, 1937, p. 32)

A Native American Empire
page 14: "And other Indians… The danger from…" (*Before and After Jamestown: Virginia's Powhatans and Their Predecessors,* pp. 38-45)

All That Glitters
page 16: "Artifacts from an Indian site…" (*Paspahegh Archaeology,* James River Institute for Archaeology, 1994); page 16: "Archaeologists can tell…" ("Demand, Supply, and Elasticity in the Copper Trade at Early Jamestown," by Seth Mallios & Shane Emmett, *Journal of the Jamestown Rediscovery Center,* Vol. 2, Jan. 2004); page 16: "Copper may also..." ("Articles of Exchange or Ingredients of New World Metallurgy?" by Carter C. Hudgins, *Early American Studies,* Spring 2005, pp. 32-64)

Nothing to Lose
page 22: Smith (*The General History: The Third Book*, Chapter 7, as reprinted in *Jamestown Narratives,* p. 290); page 23: Spelman (*Relation of Virginia,* by Henry Spelman, 1609, as reprinted in *Jamestown Narratives,* p. 482)

Indians at the Fort
page 25: "When archaeologists found..." (*Jamestown Rediscovery 7,* by William M. Kelso, J. and Beverly Straube, Association for the Preservation of Virginia Antiquities, 2001, pp. 48-49); page 25: "… Indians may have lived at the fort" (*Jamestown Rediscovery 7,* pp. 46-47)

The Dying Times
page 27: Smith (*The General History: The Third Book,* as reprinted in *Jamestown Narratives,* p. 225); page 28: Brewster (Letter from Virginia, by William Brewster, 1607, as reprinted in *Jamestown Narratives,* p. 127); page 28: Percy, "Our men were destroyed" (Observations, 1606, by George Percy, as reprinted in *Jamestown Narratives,* p. 99); page 29: "The colonists were drinking"

("Environment, Disease, and Mortality in Early Virginia," by Carville Earle, *Journal of Historical Geography,* Vol. 5, No. 4, Oct. 1979, pp. 365-390); page 29: Percy, "Our drink [was] cold water" (Discourse, as reprinted in *Jamestown Narratives,* p. 100); pages 29–30: "Later, to protect…" ("Articles, lawes, and orders, divine, politic, and martial, for the colony in Virginia," by Thomas Gates, May 24, 1610, as reprinted in *Jamestown Narratives,* p. 30); page 31: Percy, "Many through extreme…" (*A True Relation,* by George Percy, as reprinted in *Jamestown Narratives,* p. 507); page 31: "Malnourished, weak…" ("Apathy and Death in Early Jamestown," by Karen Ordahl Kupperman, *Journal of American History,* Vol. 66, No. 1 (June 1979), pp. 24-40)

Discovering the Drought
page 32: "To figure out…" ("The lost colony and Jamestown droughts," by David W. Stahle, et. al., *Science,* Vol. 280, Issue 5363, April 24, 1998, pp. 564-567)

Green Gold
page 36: "A ship captain wrote…" (*Minutes of the Council and General Court of Colonial Virginia,* edited by H.R. McIlwaine, Richmond, 1924, p. 82, as quoted in *American Slavery, American Freedom,* p. 129); page 36: "Thirty two African 'servants' …" ("The Virginia Census of 1619," by William Thorndale, *Magazine of Virginia Genealogy,* Vol. 22, No. 3, 1995, pp. 155-170); page 36: "Around 20 slaves…" ("New Light on the '20 and Odd Negroes' Arriving in Virginia, August 1619," by Engel Sluiter, *William and*

Mary Quarterly, 3rd Series, Vol. 54, No. 2, April 1997, pp. 395-398, and "The African Experience of the '20 and Odd Negroes' Arriving in Virginia in 1619," by John Thornton, *The William and Mary Quarterly,* 3rd Series, Vol. 55, No. 3, July 1998, 421-434); page 37: "…a 'young, handsome..." ("Wives for Virginia, 1621," by David R. Ransome, *William and Mary Quarterly,* 3rd Series, Vol. 48, No. 1, Jan. 1991, pp. 3-18); page 37: "For many years the settlement…" ("Women in Early Jamestown," by Kathleen M. Brown, Virtual Jamestown, Jamestown Interpretive Essays)

Winners Take All
page 39: "They struck suddenly…" (Voyage of Anthony Chester to Virginia, Made in the Year 1620, Peter Vander Aa, Bookseller, Leyden, 1707, as posted on Virtual Jamestown); page 41: Frethorne (Letter by Richard Frethorne, 1623, Virginia Company Records, as posted on Virtual Jamestown); "Within a year, Frethorne himself died" ("The Politics of Pathos," by Emily Rose, in *Envisioning an English Empire,* p. 108); page 41: Waterhouse (*A Declaration of the State of the Colony in Virginia,* by Edward Waterhouse, London, 1622, as quoted in *Envisioning an English Empire,* p. 231)

A New Look at Jamestown
page 44: "Here are some of the words..." (*Before and After Jamestown,* pp. 234-235, and *Jamestown Narratives,* pp. 70-82)

Green glass replicas of a pharma and a brandy glass.

47

Index

Illustrations are indicated by boldface.

One of the world's largest nonprofit scientific and educational organizations, the National Geographic Society was founded in 1888 "for the increase and diffusion of geographic knowledge." Fulfilling this mission, the Society educates and inspires millions every day through its magazines, books, television programs, videos, maps and atlases, research grants, the National Geographic Bee, teacher workshops, and innovative classroom materials. The Society is supported through membership dues, charitable gifts, and income from the sale of its educational products. This support is vital to National Geographic's mission to increase global understanding and promote conservation of our planet through exploration, research, and education. For more information, please call 1-800-NGS LINE (647-5463) or write to the following address:

NATIONAL GEOGRAPHIC SOCIETY
1145 17th Street N.W.
Washington, D.C. 20036-4688 U.S.A.

Visit the Society's Web site:
www.nationalgeographic.com